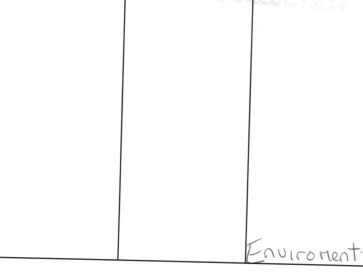

Enviroment.

Published in 2016 by Ruby Tuesday Books Ltd.

Editor: Mark J. Sachner
Designer: Emma Randall
Consultant: Judy Wearing, PhD, BEd
Production: John Lingham

Photo credits
Alamy: 25, 27 (top); Corbis: 18 (top); FLPA: 9 (right), 11 (bottom), 12–13, 16 (left), 17, 28; Public Domain: 14; Shutterstock: Cover, 2–3, 4–5, 6–7, 8, 9 (left), 10, 11 (top), 15, 16 (right), 18 (bottom), 19, 20–21, 22–23, 24, 25 (bottom left), 26, 27 (bottom), 29, 30–31.

J577.3

British Library Cataloguing in Publication Data (CIP)
is available for this title.

ISBN 978-1-910549-75-9

Printed in India

www.rubytuesdaybooks.com

Contents

Words shown in **bold** in the text are explained in the glossary.

Welcome to the Woodland

Who and what lives in the woods?

This **habitat** is home to trees, moss and **fungi**.

The residents of this habitat include squirrels, birds, spiders and other animals.

Every living thing in the woodland gets what it needs to live from its habitat.

A woodland is a type of ecosystem. An ecosystem includes all the living things in an area. It also includes non-living things such as soil, rocks, sunlight and rain. Everything in an ecosystem has its own part to play.

So let's find out what happens in this natural habitat...
...welcome to the woodland!

Acorns, Shoots, Leaves and Roots

It's spring in the woods, and fat buds are growing on the branches of trees.

When the buds burst open, leaves uncurl from inside.

If you visit a woodland, you might not notice the soil. Without it, however, the trees and other plants could not live. Plants take in water and **nutrients** from soil through their roots.

Bud

Oak tree leaves

These tree roots grow deep into the soil.

Rainwater soaks into the soil.

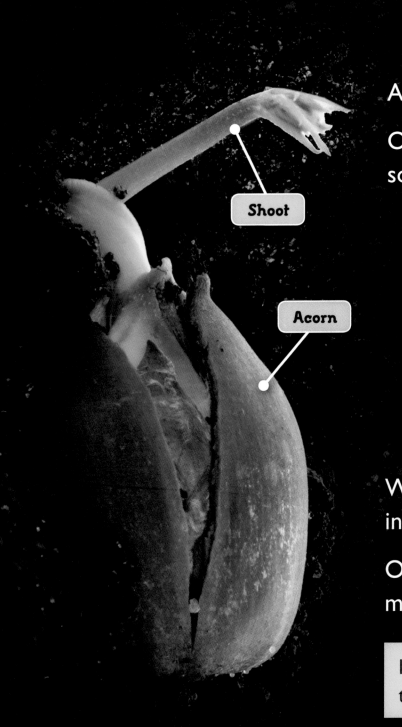

Shoot

Acorn

An acorn is buried in the soil.

Once the spring sunshine warms the soil, a **shoot** starts to grow.

Seedling

Within a few weeks, the shoot grows into an oak tree seedling.

Once the oak tree is fully grown, it may live for hundreds of years!

In what ways do you think the trees in the woodland are helpful to animals?

Tree Trunk Nests

Nest hole

Woodpecker

Peck. Peck. Peck. A female woodpecker is pecking a nest hole in a tree trunk.

Her partner helps with the work.

Once the nest is ready, the woodpecker will lay her eggs inside.

Parent woodpeckers take it in turn to sit on their eggs. The eggs must be kept warm so the chicks inside can grow.

In another tree trunk, a squirrel has found a cosy hole and made it her nest.

Inside the nest, she gives birth to four tiny babies, called kits.

She feeds the kits with milk from her body.

Mother squirrel feeding kits

Where else do animals live in a woodland?

Life Beneath the Trees

Deer

Many woodland animals live on the ground beneath the trees.

Deer move quietly through the woods, feeding on leaves, shoots, grasses, berries, seeds and fungi.

A slow worm hunts for slugs, worms and insects under logs and fallen leaves.

Slow worm

Slow worms look like small snakes, but they are actually legless lizards. They grow to about 50 cm long.

Badgers dig large underground homes called setts.

As night falls, a badger family leaves its sett to search for worms to eat.

Entrance to sett

Badger

What other animals hunt for food in the woods at night?

The Woods at Night

As night falls, many woodland creatures go looking for food.

A tiny dormouse clambers through tree branches searching for buds, seeds, berries and insects.

Dormouse

Berries

Tawny owl

Chick

A tawny owl hunts for mice, frogs and small birds.

She catches a mouse and feeds it to her chick.

Bat

A bat can eat 3000 gnats in one night!

Bats fly through the darkness hunting for moths and tiny flies called gnats.

What do ants use for building nests in a woodland?

Woodland Minibeasts

A woodland is home to millions of insects and spiders.

Wolf spider

Grasshopper

Wolf spiders hunt insects by hiding on the woodland floor and then pouncing on their **prey**.

Wood ants build an underground nest of tunnels and rooms.

Above the nest they build a huge mound of material they find in the woodland.

Wood ant

Nest mound

A nest may be home to 250,000 ants!

The mound above a wood ant nest keeps the nest warm and protects it from rain. The mound is made from the needle-like leaves of **evergreen** trees, small twigs, dried grass and moss.

What woodland birds are hunting for insects to feed to their chicks?

Hungry Babies

In the tree hole nest, the woodpecker chicks have hatched from their eggs.

The parent woodpeckers catch insects to feed to the chicks.

The adult woodpeckers eat insects and seeds.

Woodpecker chick

Father woodpecker

Nest

The squirrel kits are now seven weeks old.

When their mother leaves the nest to find food, the kits go, too.

A squirrel kit eating fungi

Squirrels eat leaves, shoots, roots, flowers and seeds. They also feed on tree bark and fungi.

Fungi

When a woodland animal dies, what do you think happens to its body?

Becoming Part of the Woodland

A deer has died in the woods.

Now, the deer's body will become food for other animals.

A fox visits the body and eats some meat.

Flies and beetles lay their eggs on the body.

When fly and beetle **larvae** hatch from the eggs, they feed on the body, too.

Fly larvae

In time, the body breaks down and rots until all that's left are bones.

Tiny bits of a rotting body get mixed into the soil. They add nutrients to the soil that plants need to grow and be healthy. Plants take in the nutrients with their roots.

Fungi help with recycling in a woodland. What do you think they recycle?

Woodland Fungi

Dead, rotting tree trunk

When a tree dies, fungi, such as mushrooms, grow on the tree.

The fungi get nutrients from the dead tree.

Fungi

As fungi spread and feed on a dead tree, they make the wood rot and become crumbly.

In time, the rotting wood becomes part of the soil.

When the wood is recycled into soil, it adds nutrients that living trees and other plants need.

Fungi

Some types of fungi grow on dead wood. Others grow on live trees, and some grow in soil. Many fungi are poisonous. So never touch fungi you see growing in a woodland, field or any other outdoor place.

What tiny plant grows on tree trunks, branches, rotting logs and rocks?

A Carpet of Moss

In a cool, damp woodland, moss grows on many trees, logs and rocks.

A carpet-like covering of moss is made up of thousands of tiny plants.

Moss

Each individual moss plant has a single stem and tiny leaves.

Moss is useful to many woodland creatures.

Insects and spiders take shelter in moss.

Mice, birds and other animals collect soft moss to put in their nests.

Water bear

Mouse

Water bears, or moss piglets, are **microscopic** animals that live in moss. A clump of moss the size of a muffin can be home to 100,000 of these creatures!

What do the woodland trees produce in summer?

A Time for Seeds

It's late summer, and the trees in the woodland have grown seeds.

Acorns drop from the oak trees.

Acorns

Spiky case

Chestnut seed

Shiny, brown chestnut tree seeds fall to the ground inside spiky cases.

Some of the seeds will one day grow into new trees.

Others become food for mice, squirrels, deer and birds.

Squirrels bury acorns and other seeds in the ground. In winter, when it's hard to find seeds, they dig up this stored food. Squirrels don't find all the seeds, though, so many grow into new trees.

A squirrel burying an acorn

Acorn

What else drops from trees in autumn?

Autumn in the Woods

When autumn arrives, the leaves on many trees turn yellow, orange, red and brown.

Soon, the leaves start to fall from the trees.

Millipedes on the ground munch on dead leaves.

Their leafy poo, which is filled with nutrients, gets mixed into the soil.

In time, the autumn leaves will rot and become new soil.

Millipede

Some of the trees are evergreens. These trees don't lose all their leaves, or needles, in autumn. Instead, they lose and regrow some of their leaves all year round.

Evergreen tree needles

What do you think the woodland deer eat in the winter?

Winter Comes Around

It's winter and snow is falling in the woodland.

There's not much to eat, so deer nibble on twigs and tree bark.

During winter, many of the woodland trees look as if they have died. They are just resting, though. In spring, they will grow new shoots and leaves.

A squirrel digs in the snow.

It's looking for buried
acorns and other seeds.

For now the woodland is still and white.
But soon it will be spring again....

A Woodland Food Web

A food web shows who eats who in a habitat.

This food web diagram shows the connections between some of the living things in a woodland.

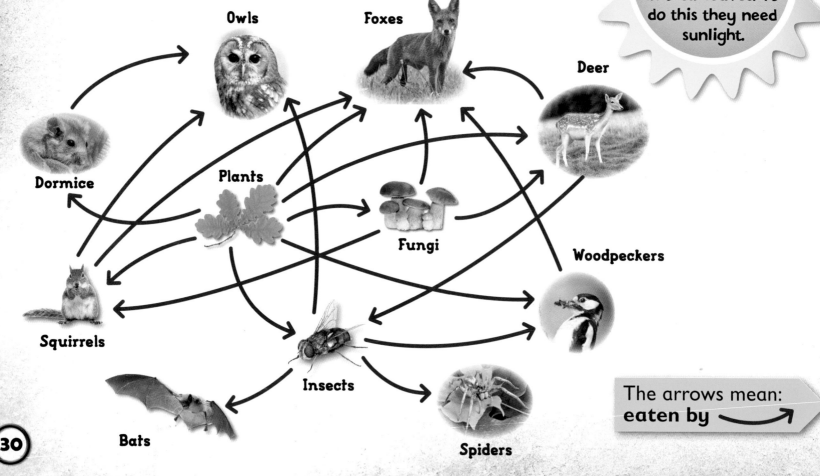

Owls

Foxes

Deer

Dormice

Plants

Fungi

Woodpeckers

Squirrels

Insects

Bats

Spiders

The arrows mean: eaten by

Glossary

evergreen
Having green leaves all year round.

fungi
A group of living things that includes mushrooms, toadstools and moulds.

habitat
The place where living things, such as animals and plants, live and grow. Woodlands, gardens and deserts are all types of habitats.

larva
A young insect that looks like a worm.

microscopic
Able to be seen only with a microscope, not with the eyes alone.

nutrient
A substance that a living thing needs to grow, get energy and be healthy.

prey
An animal that is hunted by other animals for food.

shoot
A new part that grows on a plant or from a seed. Shoots can become new stems or leaves.

Index

Learn More Online

To learn more about life in a woodland, go to
www.rubytuesdaybooks.com/habitats